FISHING

Bruno Broughton

The Bookwright Press
New York • 1991

Flying Start

Titles in this series

Fishing   Running
Gymnastics   Soccer
Judo   Swimming

Words in **bold** in the text are explained in the glossary on page 30.

Cover: Fishing is a popular sport all around the world.

First published in the
United States in 1991 by
The Bookwright Press
387 Park Avenue South
New York, NY 10016

First published in 1991 by
Wayland (Publishers) Ltd
61 Western Rd, Hove
East Sussex BN3 1JD, England

Library of Congress Cataloging-in-Publication Data
Broughton, Bruno.
    Fishing/Bruno Broughton.
        p.   cm. —— (Flying start)
    Includes bibliographical references and index.
    Summary: Describes the varieties, techniques, and safety factors
of fishing.
    ISBN 0-531-18432-3
    1. Fishing – Juvenile literature.   [1. Fishing]   I. Title.
II. Series.
SH445.B76   1991
799.1 – dc20

91–4391
CIP
AC

Typesetter: Dorchester Typesetting Group Ltd
Printer: Casterman S.A., Belgium.

CONTENTS

HOOKED ON FISHING!

Angling is great fun, because it gets you out into the fresh air, to beautiful places full of interesting fish. You can go with a group of friends and make your trip an expedition. You could take lunch with you and go for the whole day.

While you are trying to catch fish, you might spot some of the animals and plants that live in and by water. So keep your eyes peeled.

Left Fishing takes you to beautiful places you might not see otherwise.

Left This woman has caught three big fish in one afternoon.

You will make new friends when you start trying to catch fish — **anglers** like to help each other and will give you useful tips on how to become a better angler.

To begin with, you will probably want to catch whatever comes along. Later on, you might decide to specialize in catching extra large **trophy fish**, or to go after trout or salmon. Or you could try for some ocean fish, which are very tasty!

Left You meet a lot of people when you take up fishing, as you can see from this picture.

Many anglers like to compete against others. If you are very skilled, you might one day decide you would like to compete in a professional fishing tournament. There, you will meet many other people who love to fish. Or you might decide that it is more fun just to see which of your group of friends can catch the biggest fish.

One of the most important parts of angling is talking to your friends about it afterward. Most people have nearly as much fun telling stories about the one that got away as they do fishing!

Whatever sort of fishing you choose, you will not be on your own. There are more than 35 million anglers in the United States and millions more in other countries.

Below Although going fishing with your friends is fun, sometimes it is good to go on your own.

ON THE RIGHT LINES

Where to go fishing

Where you go fishing will depend on where you live. Fish can be caught in rivers and streams, small ponds and large reservoirs, lakes in parks and canals . . . and in the ocean. Which of these is nearest to where you live? That is probably the best place for you to start fishing.

Left You can go fishing in lots of places. This man (and his dog!) are fishing on an Irish lough (lake).

But when you arrive, which spot will give you the best fishing? When you have learned more about the sport, you will be able to look at the water and figure out where most of the fish will be. But in the beginning, it is better to ask an experienced angler which are the best spots for you to fish from.

Above This man from Sri Lanka has built a special place to fish from. Do **not** try this yourself!

When can I go fishing?

You can fish in the ocean whenever you like. Some fish spend all their life near the seashore, by piers or harbors, or among the rocks. So these are good places to fish. Other fish come near the shore only at certain times of the year. Some of the books listed on page 31 will tell you which fish do this and at what times they come in to shore.

Left Some fish live near the seashore all year round. These fish in Darwin, Australia, will take food from people's hands.

In **fresh water** there are times of the year called **closed seasons** when you are not allowed to fish. This is to let the fish **spawn**. The closed seasons are different for **game fish**, such as trout and salmon, and others, such as roach, carp and perch.

Always check to make sure you are not fishing in the closed season.

Above Salmon travel up the river when they are about to spawn.

Do I need permission?

If you fish in fresh water in the United States you will probably have to buy a **fishing license**. This lets you fish in your state. If you are fishing in another state, you may need another fishing license that lets you fish in that state.

Below You can buy a fishing license, as well as equipment, in a fishing **tackle** shop.

Left This man looks as though he is trying to hide from the license inspector! In fact, he is just making sure he does not scare the fish away.

If you are below a certain age (16 in most states), you do not need a fishing license.

If the land you are fishing from is owned by someone, you will need a permit. Often, you can buy a permit for a day's fishing. Sometimes you can join an angling club and buy a

Left You do not need a license to fish in the ocean, although the owner of a pier might make you buy a ticket.

season permit, which lasts most of the year. Sometimes, you can even fish for free!

Make sure you have your permit before you go fishing, or find out if you can buy one when you get there.

You do not need a fishing license or a permit to fish in the ocean. See page 31 for books that contain local fishing regulations, or write to your State Game and Fish Commission.

Will fishing cost much?

Fishing is not expensive. A fishing license is very cheap or maybe even free! And your permit – if you need one – is unlikely to cost much either.

When you begin, you do not need a lot of equipment. The things you do need will not cost very much. Most anglers add to their tackle later, as they become more experienced.

Left You do not need a lot of equipment to go fishing. This boy has caught a fish with a cheap rod and reel.

FISHING SKILLS

Knowing about fish

The more you know about different kinds of fish, the better you will be at fishing. You can learn more about fish from books about them. The books listed on page 31 will start you off.

Many kinds of fish are found in fresh water. Some – such as carp – can grow to over 45 pounds (20 kg) and may live for thirty years!

Left A carp, one of the hardest fish to catch.

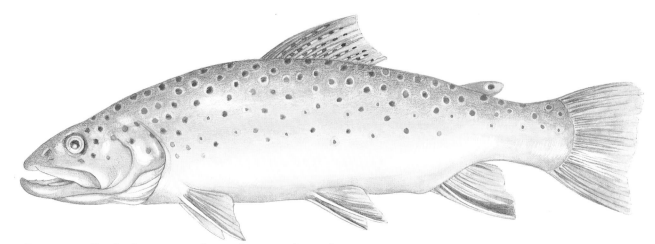

Game fish live in fresh and salt water. Trout breed naturally in rivers and streams. But to make sure that there are enough trout to be caught, fish are sometimes reared on trout farms and put into fishing waters. Salmon live in the ocean for most of their lives. They **migrate** into rivers in order to lay their eggs.

There are lots of different ocean fish. Some of them weigh twice as much as a full-grown person! Cod, flounder, tuna, grouper and sharks are among the fish regularly caught in the ocean.

A trout.

Below This boy has caught a dogfish, which is a kind of shark.

Tackle for the job

You do not need to buy a lot of expensive equipment to start with. You just need a rod and reel, some line and hooks, and a few weights and floats. You also need a disgorger, or "hook-out," which is a metal or plastic tool that helps you unhook a fish without hurting it. Take one along whenever you go fishing.

When you buy your fishing tackle, always ask the advice of your fishing tackle dealer – he or she will help you decide what is the best tackle for the waters you want to fish in.

What about bait?

To catch fish, anglers use some sort of food, or bait, to tempt them to bite on the hook. Bait can be real food, either alive or dead. It can also be an imitation, which tricks the fish.

Below This hook has been baited with bloodworm.

For many freshwater fish, your bait could be bread, cheese or many of the things you eat yourself. You can collect worms or buy crickets from the tackle shop.

Ocean fish are caught on strips of fish, squid or special sea worms, such as sandworm and bloodworm.

Above Maggots are a good bait.

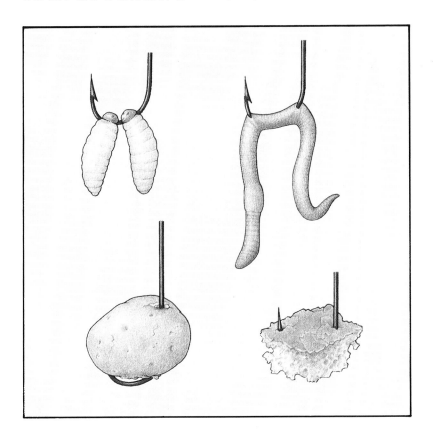

Left Different baits — maggots, worm, bread and potato.

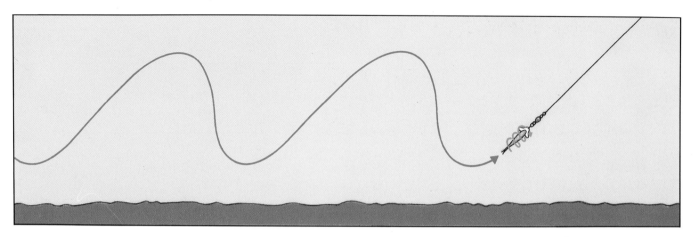

Above and **right** All artificial baits work by darting about like fish.

When fly-fishing for trout and salmon, you use an artificial fly made of silk, fur or feathers. You can buy flies from tackle shops or make your own — fly-tying is lots of fun and a challenge.

When you are fishing for **predatory fish** such as pike you might use plastic or metal **lures**. These flash and wiggle like real fish and trick the predator into attacking.

Knots – the vital link

Fishing line is quite smooth and you will need to learn how to tie special knots that do not slip. Your tackle will include at least one knot, to connect your line to your hook.

Always make the line wet before tightening the knot. Test the knot by pulling from both sides before you start fishing.

Below A knot you can use to tie your hook onto your fishing line.

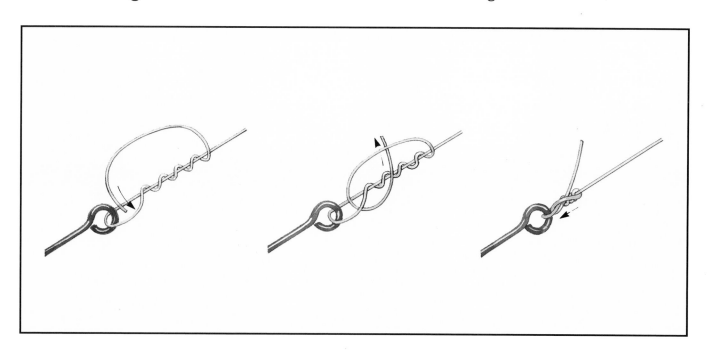

Learning to cast

If you can cast well you will be able to place your bait where you see fish or expect them to be. Unless you can do that, you do not stand much chance of catching any fish!

Casting is not hard, but you do need to practice. Learn how to handle your tackle and cast properly before you go fishing. The best place to learn is in a field, using a weight (but not a hook!) on the end of your line. Make sure there is no one nearby whom you could hit with the weight.

Left Anglers who go fly-fishing have to be very good at casting.

Keep it clean!

You should always try to follow this advice, otherwise you may not be able to go back and fish again.

- make sure you have permission to fish and obey fishery rules.
- never leave any litter – take it home with you. Otherwise you spoil other people's enjoyment.
- do not light fires.
- respect the countryside – do not disturb wildlife or damage water plants.
- always close gates and keep to paths across farm land.
- report any **pollution** – the people to contact may be shown on your fishing license or permit.
- treat fish carefully – wet your hands before touching them and never throw them back: place them gently in the water.

Above The effect of dropping litter. **Below** Fishing in this river would be impossible – all the fish are dead.

SAFETY

Fishing is a very safe sport but you **must** be careful when you are near water. Learn to swim first – it could save your life.

There are some simple safety rules that you should follow when you go fishing:

1   Make sure you tell someone older where you are going fishing and what time you will get back. It is a good idea to go fishing with a friend or group of friends.

2   Always fish where it is safe – avoid slippery rocks and watch out for overhanging banks.

3   Unless you are **certain** that it is very shallow at the water's edge,

Below Do not fish from slippery, wet riverbanks. It is very dangerous.

do not wade into the water. Never wade into fast or deep water.

4 **Do not** fish from a boat on your own and **always** wear a life jacket when afloat.

5 **Never swim in fishing waters** – the water is often cold, you may get tangled in water weeds, and there may be strong currents.

6 Take notice of warning signs – they are there for your safety.

Left Do not wade into the water unless you are sure it is shallow and there is someone who could help if you fell over.

FISHING WITH AN EXPERT

Luck plays a part in most sports, including angling. However, a good angler prepares for a day's fishing well ahead and uses his or her skill to outwit the fish. Here is an example of how an expert tackles one type of fishing.

Left Some fish are difficult to land. This one is struggling very hard.

Lure fishing for pike

The expert knows that there are fish as long as your arm in the lake and chooses strong tackle! The rod is 10 feet (3 m) long and the reel has line on it that can hold a very heavy fish. A wire **leader** is tied at the end of the fishing line, to stop a pike from biting through the line with its sharp teeth.

The bait is a spinner, a metal lure that flashes as it is wound in. The angler picks a spot facing the wind – this is often one of the best places to fish from.

Above The pike is sometimes called the freshwater shark because of its sharp bite.

There is a swirl on the surface and the spinner is cast to the right spot. There is a firm pull on the line, the fish strikes! The angler gives a jerk to **set the hook**.

The pike pulls the line out so quickly that the rod bends! This will tire it out. When it is tired, the line can be wound in a little, before the fish rushes off again. Gradually, it is **played** to the bank and scooped up in the landing net.

The pike is unhooked quickly, using a long, metal disgorger, or "hook-out." The angler then wets his hands, to avoid damaging the fish, and weighs it in a soft, wet bag. At 22 pounds (10 kg), it is a trophy fish!

Three photographs are taken – the pike is big enough to be reported to the fishing newspapers. The angler then puts the pike back gently and it swims away. Now someone else

Below A large pike that weighed 22 pounds (10 kg).

may catch it. Perhaps the same person might even catch it again. Next time, though, the pike will be a bit wiser and harder to catch!

Left Put fish back carefully – never throw them.

Glossary

Angler   A person who goes fishing for fun.

Angling   Going out and trying to catch fish for fun.

Closed season   The time of year during which you are not allowed to fish. This is so that the fish can breed.

Fishing license   A paper that gives you permission to fish in a particular area.

Fresh water   Water that is not salty, such as rivers and lakes.

Game fish   An edible fish that can give sport to the angler.

Leader   A piece of line or wire at the end of the tackle.

Lure   An artificial bait. It can be called either a spinner, spoon or plug.

Migrate   Change the place in which you live. When salmon migrate they go from the ocean to the river.

Play   To play a fish into the bank is to move it gradually in that direction.

Pollution   Dirt and impurity. Oil spilled in the ocean is a form of pollution.

Predatory fish   A fish that eats other fish.

Season permit   A paper that gives you permission to fish for a whole season in one place. The season is the time of year that fish do not breed.

Setting the hook   The movement of jerking the rod quickly backward to hook a fish.

Spawn   To lay eggs that will hatch into baby fish.

Stringer   A piece of line used to keep caught fish in the water.

Tackle Fishing equipment, such as hooks and floats.
Trophy fish A fish that is particularly large in comparison with other fish of the same kind.

Books about fishing

For fishing regulations: *The Sportsman's Almanac* by Corley Farquhar, Harper & Row, New York, 1965

A Complete Guide to Fishing by Vlad Evanoff, Thomas Y. Crowell Company, New York, 1961

Fishing by John F. Waters, Franklin Watts, New York/London, 1978

Fishing Basics by John Randolph, Prentice-Hall, Inc., Englewood Cliffs, New Jersey, 1981

Freshwater Fish & Fishing by Jim Arnosky, Four Winds Press, New York, 1982

The next step

Some organizations offering information for young anglers include:

American Bass Association
886 Trotters Trail,
Wetumpka, AL 36092

American Casting Association
1739 Praise Blvd.,
Fenton, MO 63026

Bass'n Gal
P.O. Box 13925,
2007 Roosevelt,
Arlington, TX 76013

Brotherhood of the Jungle Cock
P.O. Box 576,
Glen Burnie, MD 21061

Future Fisherman Foundation
Highway 9,
Spirit Lake,
IA 51360

Great Lakes Sport Fishing Council
293 Berteau,
Elmhurst, IL 60126

Index

Numbers in **bold** indicate pictures or artwork as well as text.

Picture Acknowledgments

Brian and Cherry Alexander 8, 11, 12, 22; All-Sport (A Murrell) 6, 13; Angling Photo Source 16, 19; Chapel Studios 4, 15, 18; Eye Ubiquitous *cover*, 10; Chris Fairclough 7; Oxford Scientific Films 5, 25, 26, 28; Mick Toomer 17, 29; Tim and Jenny Woodcock 14, 21; Zefa 9, 23 (both).

Artwork supplied by Andrew Popkiewicz (RT Partners).